THE WORK OF THE WIND

THE WORK OF THE WIND

S.J. Litherland

FlambardPress

First published in Great Britain in 2006 by Flambard Press
Stable Cottage, East Fourstones, Hexham NE47 5DX
www.flambardpress.co.uk

'Coda' from *Collected Poems* by Louis MacNeice (Faber)
reproduced by kind permission

Typeset by Book Type
Cover Design by Gainford Design Associates
Front cover image: Detail from 'Burning Books: Study II',
ink and wash by Rachel Levitas
Printed in Great Britain by Cromwell Press, Trowbridge, Wiltshire

A CIP catalogue record for this book
is available from the British Library.
ISBN-13: 978-1-873226-82-7
ISBN-10: 1-873226-82-9

Flambard Press wishes to thank Arts Council England
for its financial support.

Flambard Press is a member of Inpress,
and of Independent Northern Publishers.

CONTENTS

for Barry MacSweeney

CODA

Maybe we knew each other better
When the night was young and unrepeated
And the moon stood still over Jericho.

So much for the past; in the present
There are moments caught between heart-beats
When maybe we know each other better.

But what is that clinking in the darkness?
Maybe we shall know each other better
When the tunnels meet beneath the mountain.

Louis MacNeice

I

UNWRITTEN ENTRIES

POETRY AS A CHINESE JAR MOVING
IN ITS STILLNESS

We were talking of poetry. Eliot and Stevens. Your eyes
were yellow-gold of a bee's blur, arresting on my idea.
Your lip demurred: What interests me now is smashing the jar.

The fragments. Sunday, we drove to uplands of Autumn. You,
for the first time, in the driver's seat, cautiously
changing gear. The moors witnessing the L-plates.

I was so proud of your caution: the poet diffident
and responsible. A new man. New wings. Not crashing
from bed to floor with the sudden fit like rain on the moor,

the tell-tale temple bruise. The mark of self-murder.
Monday, the jar was too complete, moving in its stillness.
With intuitive discord you tested the harmony,

rang a warning. The hurled cup did not break, the tipped
over golden basted duck and gravy only spattered my coat.
Upstairs the once cracked clock had stopped, its window

of postcards ribboned and scored, augmented by your lover's
surge of words, waited for deliverance into fragments.
The wrenching apart of quotation marks. A better poetry.

The despoiler of balance still moves in his shaking.
The eternal jar is reassembling piece by piece.
The idea of order is presiding over the nature of fragments.

UNDER COVER

          Doubt like marsh gas,
happiness brief flower
               checked
peace softening us
            while in the bag
a quiet bomb
            empty of its violence,
in your veins lethal juice.

          Yet I took it on
for the sake of your fresh
pressed flower face
            after making love.
For the stolen boy.
             The poison ultra-strong
reluctant to leave
            only love more tenacious.

          You stayed up all night
patrolled the grass
            crashed through
the second fence
            each perimeter the years
grew
   a well-ringed journey.
              It takes
no time at all to slip back
            and every
pace forward a charging of wire.
                If
you rest on this plateau, rest.
The night unwinds, unlike death.

AT BAY

Whips are out, they're to hand
                         ferocity comes
easy
   the backbeat of pity
                acid in her face
(if you dodge it
      forget it
you're not fit for tribal warfare).

                 Absolute black
the goad is the limit
           she'll snap back
snap at last
      turn with instinct.
We're out
      of territorial waters
even the water broken
               smashed like glass.
There's nothing to stop us falling.

                 Absolute night
doesn't last.
    It's prey to light
and ordinary behaviour
            craves return to small moves
the pawns on the board,
         the damned important pawn.
Not only queen and my soul's king move
              also the retinue.

SWAN IN LOVE

Eyes lit with lust, in you gold dust,
pollen, eyes seeking daylight.

Everything featureless. Newborn.
There's a jetstream in my heart and loins.

We're inside out, hearts on sleeves.
I should have suspected those sinews,

those dominating eyes, the flexing
of that perfect mouth sitting like a plum

to be eaten, stamping *will* across my brow.
Wings in shadows, you were never anything

but swan. This one will bleed your heart
effortlessly. Fate

on cue. No apologies.
Fierce tightener of all screws.

There's no chance to pause, devourer
of daybreak, of all forms of sleep.

Drag me through the richest turmoil.
Your jumbled up hate, the spit and hiss.

Your eyes humbled in delayed weakness.
Love unkits the armour. How did you save

all that nakedness, still flesh, still fire?
You kept the ardour untrimmed, kept it

from decay, kept it from the scales.
Not prepared to swap it *anytime*

for peace, and the seductive kiss
on my neck is bloodlust and gold dust.

DESIRE

You're sick, so sick the careful meal is overthrown.
You have to run and in the mêlée the clock is broken
and stops, its glass cracked across. You blame

the lake of wine, and I think of Lucifer, fallen
and chained. *A drink*, you mutter. *A drink. A drink.*

Your eyes circle, protrude. *You'll be sick*; I refuse.

Your eyes stand out, stare out, chained to your lake.
You don't understand. I must have a drink. A drink.

Your lips are dry, dry as dust, your eyes forced out
of their sockets. You shiver, twitch, shiver, raddled
by an invisible sieve. In you is something animal

stirring. Out comes your tongue. It sticks out, lolls,
pants, looks round, your tongue is looking round
as if it had an eye. *A drink. I want a drink.*

A chorus of the damned, an incantation of the damned,
your eyes now wholly a desperate animal chained up
inexplicably. *It's terrible*, you moan, and

you become the dog and pant, your tongue far out,
panting violently like a dog after a run, your eyes
roaming like the eyes of the mad, or a dog after

he's home and wants relief from thirst. *A drink.*

MOVING AROUND LIKE PLANETS

Our first bed, darkness in the dark room. Booze
sweating out of you like paint stripper, and I

clinging onto the intuitive conversing of our bodies,
veins humming like telephone wires over dark stretches

of countryside. The recognition of likeness, and you,
over marshes of doubt, take my hand and press it

into your heart. You were deeply entangled in the thicket –
on your brow the spangled crown of eczema.

>*I'm in my ravaged corner, friendless on the hard floor.*
How did you get under the wire of my boneyard?

Weeping for ten years' solitary and we hang on
the whole night under a castaway eiderdown.

Our second bed in the light of your best bedroom, lovingly
decorated with a vase of buttercups, under the fresh new

covers of the unwrapped, just bought, duvet. And you,
fingering my bones like a surgeon, delicately, chastely,

counting the notches of my spine, angles of my shoulder,
notations of my wrists, as if I were an altar you wanted

to bless, your eyes priestly. Our third bed.
My hand slips under the wire of your clothes.

There's a jerk and a groan from you, kick of light, kicking
to the surface. You swam up from the dark pool and washed

my face in kisses, swam over me entirely.
>*Testicles moving around like planets*, you say.

THE CIRCLE

On the water a left movement, a trickle curling.
It's not absolutely still.

He's flying to his destiny, burden shed.
Everything's cast off, the water kicked off, the swan-run

over you as he strides up, neck rigid, eyes straining.
Only flight matters. When he's up he'll remember

you and the forged dream of ordinary happiness,
the smallest of doors into the enchanted garden full of fears

and wayward plots, laid waste, pain beaten out of town by drums.

Instinct says, *Return.* Retrace the air to her.
The land's burnt below. There must be a twig somewhere

to lodge in his beak, a gift of love immutable.

Return. The necessity in his brain.
He has to come down, past all the signs that said

Get Out! Tears hard as bloodstones are offered
to cancel calamitous threats.

SWAN IN THE WEEDS

I thought betrayal an intense thing. It's slight.
I walk to the Co-op. Buy three bottles of white.
       The sober thing so dearly bought, the wine so cheaply.

For a day, I honoured my sobriety and lit
two candles, close together as I could fit,
       touching on sand. Thanksgiving for a day.

On the second day I announced my sobriety.
I stood undefiled, unprotected but with
       a responsible person (I am not responsible).

On the third day, just before closing, I entered
the Co-op. No mistake about what I wanted this time.
       I was completely sober, my dear. Nothing remains,

destruction is quick, a cheap exit. You can never say
I didn't choose the wine over you. Pure preference.
       Yes, I deceived you about the light. As you leave,

leave me in the dark. You lost the final encounter.
Look at the state of the world. I'm back in bed, drunk.

       I slipped the cork, I drank the white knowledge.

DON'T REPEAT LITTLE

You have a little wee voice. *Don't repeat little.*
You have a correcting voice. It's the same sing-song.
It's sung somewhere in your drunken head, sly

and silky with complaint. You are a little boy grown
old, chanting nonsense like a little boy to shut out
what you're being told. Hullo, you say, welcome

to my special hell where I repeat everything
I've said before and drown out voices. I'm ill

so you'll excuse me as I read my poem, sing my song,
or snarl as I want, I want, I want. *Don't*
interrupt. I'll bark you down. And my voice is slush,

skidding over words now, running and falling, sliding.
It's unravelled in my head where you can't detect
the lie, the everlasting lie, I must tell.

I'm a child. Don't scold. Don't scold. *Aaaaaaarggh!*
The phone goes cold. It's your nightly drunken lullaby.

IF I ONLY HAD SOMEONE TO PROTECT ME

Your face not quite clean, your scalp
not quite clean, you sit demurely,

face exposed by new razoring not quite
perfect, orbited by plates of old food,

the ignored brown envelopes
silting the carpet by the letterbox.

Your smell doesn't compete, but it's there,
personal and stale, tinged with the soiled

navy T-shirt you've lived and slept in
and the tartan jacket never taken off.

Until this time my love always
so clean, washed and powdered, in newly

ironed garments, with daily shampooed
hair and fetishly polished shoes,

he's grimed and sweated to the smell
of old flowers stuck in old flower water.

From the corners only bottles gleam,
line the stair like torches to the dark room.

Before you shut the door I see rankings
of them closing round your chair like mould

over your food. You're not aware of your
toilet's stench, blissfully happy I'm here,

drunk on love and just drunk, the alcohol
tide over your lips. In all that mess just

one spark of hope in the carefully hung
set of clean clothes. You're ready, like any

pregnant mum, to be taken into hospital.
If only the call would come. And they're

waiting for you, nurses and doctors, only
waiting for you to stop drinking and pick

up the phone, take charge and control,
as you drink on, drink on, drink on.

UNWRITTEN ENTRIES

Q. (Her) What's caused this?
A. (Anaesthetist) Ravages of alcohol.

Death waits, my mind compacted. He's chosen a lean pin
for my brain. No words left. Only chemical messages.

This could be a radio station. Space flight. Wired up, tubes in,
my heartbeat synthesized, every movement a jagged edge. Out
pours the black blood. Well rid of it. The turbulence of throwing
up. The music of machines soothes me, my drowsy words heavy
in oxygen under the mask. And here again comes the disjuncture,
inarticulation, memory violated, the jamming of all stations.

A night of blackwater rapids. The heart about to crack is lulled,
has been lulled by the heminevrin lullaby. Oh, so sweet,
the pipe is singing to me its shuttle pump. Easy, you can turn
it down. My eyes are searched with a torch. Every bell of the clock.
Where are you? I know. *What day is it?* I'll never know. And life
is sticking to me with its rods and tubes and wires. Plugged in.

It's hair-shirt time. I see it clearly. And I cannot remove it.
Because it's my skin I'm trying to lift. I pluck and pluck.

We're all prisoners in this hut, manned by guards and barbed wire.
But here's *John Prescott*, fancy that. Where's the wine? I'll miss it.
Going out for fish and chips and a pint and a half of VODKA.
The last hallucination scuttles over the floor

and I crush it with my foot. An innocent rose petal.

Death behind me. Hospital pills jingle in my pocket. They turf us
out with broken bones, my thinning skin rivalling the ozone layer
scabs under sunshine. I limp to the car. She drives my life
like an ambulance. Destination she'll offer: more of this kind.

Punishment or treatment. It's hard to distinguish and tears,
sober tears tread my cheeks slowly, they're hard, not like
easy drunken weeping, lift my lashes against the bald light.

FUTURES

Your hand not once on my breast, your tongue not once
in my mouth, quietly we paraded through the grounds,

stilted figures out of a pre-war landscape, or a
forties film where the fiancée and her flyer talk

of their future and we know his number's up.
Future. The future. It's this lonely longing

in the sun, separation while the war goes on and on.
And will you come home, beloved? Jacket slung

carefree over your shoulder, sunglasses, even a tan
your skin's learning to accept, and that slight

roguish smile on your lips, so pleased with yourself?
Can I come in? You'll say in the celluloid ending

when we clutch each other in tears. Or will you repeat
the phrase – muttered after a silent drive from

the last hospital discharge: *Now the nightmare begins.*

VICTORY

I'm just mouth talking. Made it all up inside my head.
Mouth trying to straighten itself, can't make the 's'
sound right. Try again. It's like rain dribbling

down the window. It's the clown slipping up, straightening
out his broken hat. No-one will ever notice it's crooked.
I'm still lovable, just a child with a breathless voice.

I'm playing. The lies are there to put you on track.
I know you'll hear the fizz above the gin.
I'm only here to drink and I hate your impertinence,

your panic, your self-appointed anxiety.
I'll just pretend to keep you knocking on my door.
It's shut. *Pet lamb.* Hatred shut it years ago. You're not

the first to think love's stronger. I prefer
the splendour of hatred with a passion like Hitler's.
In comparison daylight is small and domestic.

I'm with Nietzsche and the tigers. We're raking the sky
with our claws. Raking up poetry. Nothing balanced
like yours. I'm all rages. *That's me.* No kittenface.

You're just too little for my scope. I'll rampage
or lose my wings. Nerve me now for the last flight.
Yet our harmony tempted me. Tempted me down for you

to pet me. If only you could see me as I really am.
Tall adult man, slender and hip turning, hair loosened,
eyes waiting for you, passion waiting for you, as I was

at 27. Now 20 years on I'm not broken or drunken.
I'm here with my salute! Passion is my medium –
not rancour – *rising like mist towards the sun.*

NAMING

O where are you?

Barry, Barry Mac

Baz, Bazza

BAR

co-conspirator

B

Mr J'accepte

Swan

Doll, dolly-doll, doll-bird

Mr Pookah

Suprematist Heart

comrade, black moon insurrectionist

quoit spinner, planet mover

ankle twinner and twiner

award winner of Chu-chiness

face stroker

night arm shield

Dark Room Tragedian

chemise mist lover   rain adorer

postcard scribe

leaf presser

flower crusher

plant consultant (free)

herbman

cook

choice treats enthusiast

peppermint sucker

chocolate swallower

Rachel's hat syndrome adviser

BARD

kittenface, tar kitten

seraphsmiler

Title King

Hyde apologist

Wrecker

contempt cataloguer

Futurist

Irish gun runner
word dove flutterer
                    Mr Self Proclaimed Genius
Mr Self Proclaimed Nobody
Advanced Tea Maker
        Speech Perfectionist
                        Word rustler
            Musical Voice Operator
hand on the shoulder supporter
heart-stopping hipslover
tireless bone surgeon
                tireless dancer
the beautiful game maniac
breast curtain opener extraordinaire
            white stocking lacetop seeker
Mr Perfectly Clean
Talcum Silk Cock Man
                        shoe appreciation society founder
dragon of the bottle hoarde
            soup flask preparer
ex-fisherman, ex-pigman, ex-horticulturist
ex-husband-twice
 ex-lover-various
POET
 striker
union delegate
    KEEPER OF THE FLAME
skin stripper
            Self Confessed Alcoholic
Drink Worshipper,
                Addiction Hater
Ravaged Corner Propagandist
                    Journalist
Self Disdained Hack
Self Proclaimed Biggest Bastard Newsdesk Cane Keeper
Captain of the Paranoia Squad
                    hater of *italics*
state of the nation bulletin proclaimer

'But of course' abolitionist
                    jibe serial killer
                taxi hailer
law trekker
Geordie lad
 black T-shirt impulse buyer
      Mr Cool in Dark Shades Customer
                        owner of the perfect mouth
pledge believer
                        doubter
Once-a-day breaker of vows
  lost child, boy, man
                Past Torturer
Self Diagnosed Othello Complex partisan
            sober golden dream man
glasses misplacer
key swapper
                            gifts dump client
against the odds de-tox struggler
best shot merchant
                poetry derider
Black Suede Boot Press non-publisher
      Bunting biography non-author
Dissenter
        grave digger of the Revolution
Temper free spender
                Door kicker
Passionate eyes endurer
                glamour star
little present surprise king

                                    angst fomenter

bomb thrower
 kitchen adroit concoction manufacturer
     vinegar collector
Malevich railway bridge fancier
would-be cyclist   would-be driver
mediocre moviedrome licensee
    gin debauchee

Peutêtre, peutêtre equivocator
Francophile
supermarket aisle swinger
L'homme of the We'll See
Threshold Stressmaker
courting tape giver and taker
black earth scorcher
Rhetorical Questionnaire Head Clerk
Quotation Marks Estranger
changeling prince
soul exchanger
espouser
Finnbar Padraig
BPM

FOR ANOTHER VALENTINE'S DAY

Matisse: Pierrot's Funeral

Scattering of demon leaves   pestilence of yellow
pink and black   white child horses uprear   white
toy horses prettily pull Pierrot's coach   upside down
hearts hang in the wheels   he's in there somewhere
in the white ghost coach   his pimpernel flower
bloodwound   sportive plume among the ferns   horses
toss and toss   the coach trundles on uneven wheels
cerise bordered   no words no Pierrot   white on black

ROSES

Single stems of pepper plants in fine ink tracery
and red lipped. My card sends anniversary

roses. Today arrives day late flowers bagged
from your garden. Red budded peony and orange

drooping poppy, thyme flowers and mint: a posy
of his mind. Love casting chances on last days.

The beauty of his gesture unshrivelled.
He's the one to throw the rose on the shrine.

The wartime films, the silver screen three times
a week, one she remembered: *Stewart Grainger*

tossing onto the dead bosom of her heroine,
gypsy and madonna, the rose lying beside the cross.

And I chose the rose. Out into the blackout streets,
the stars glistening and bristling close to the earth

said '*rose*': diamonds of the sky, everybody's gift.

And the unknown who must have stood (as I did)
behind the rails of Shakespeare's Stratford tomb,

and cast to lie aslant, between twin official urns
of stiff necked arched out flowers, a single

long stemmed leaf ragged red rose, breathing its death.

I picked up the gesture of the rose. In drunken
senility you searched for the right words,

in trammels of fog you elevated the poppy.
Weeping for forgetting. Between swallowings of tears

you said: I'll send you Arctic Roses. Unerringly
choosing the wrong word and the right gesture.

Arctic *Roses* you repeated, making sure of your footing.

THE KEENING

1

The voice kite high in the air, flies above descending
waterfalls crashing down pain, it cannot come down,
swept upward, is high, thin, remorseless, a cry
flying itself out of energy, not even searching the skies,
but finds itself flying alone, not a child's heartache
or lover's, a voice in no-man's-land pinned on the wire
keening above the blasted landscape, no way back.

2

Is it mother in me, or soul, or love tuned to the note?
The keening is new, a new rhythm, and something inside me
is not free from hearing, knows the keening is relentless,
unendurable, and she will pick up the burden like a baby
in the dream she is responsible for. The keening is this
neglected baby she has to wash, not hers, no-one's, a baby
left alone fretting and wet, cheeks scratched by tiny nails.

SPARTACUS AT 5 A.M.

Once your hour of waking for work. Downstairs the ironed shirt.
Meditative cup of tea and visit to garden. The herb inspection.

Peace. The wine din satisfied. A simple release before the wine god
demands his coin. Drink the Faustian pact: a mantle of ecstasy

and dance of the sins conjured out of nothing but weakness for
spectacle.
Nothing cheap about thrills. Faustus and his brethren, rock'n'rollers,

and the Toon Army looking into its glass at weekends and spiralling
lasses out of control. Disorder and dance and Dionysian chants.

Last nights as you enter the vortex of pleasure and pain. Pleasure
no longer ecstasy but blessed relief pursued down a tunnel.

In the morning light, before the deadly monotonous day
begins, monotony not a burden, you see coldly your damnation.

Clockwork repetition. This is your morning time for taking breath
before the chained walk to the Co-op for mind liquor to quieten

the body's sacrifice under nails. Faust pays for unearned power
and pleasure in terrible correct ratio. His screams of anguish

are the warnings no-one hinders. Faust shattered like a mirror.
Each morning you know you have survived the night. Still facing

the trodden path with less and less. You are so light now, one pair
of jeans, one T-shirt, one summer jacket, one pair of shoes.

Everything dropped to carry the burden. No phone calls out.
No distress signals. Just concentration on a fading routine

as day begins. But you've taken in with you a knife that glitters,
your self-knowledge glitters, you're not just slave but Spartacus,

when the wine god sleeps you'll cut his throat or cut out his heart
or take him like Beowulf pursuing the beast to the lake depths.

35

RED DAWN

First light gold stripes the grasses
  stretches and stresses on the grass

We're thankful it's dawn these warm bed mornings

  Outside, the clearest sky
             inside, the red room
waiting for the tree to blossom its leaves
the poison trembles its time

and the laying down of its long five years
The tree pent up for deliverance

Into the dark house, treading up stairs as though on glass,
cans ungathered, your mouth soaked like a cake on Guinness

and brandy laced, a dark beard of a week's staining, your lost
child eyes, the bawl of anger brought short   **here I am**

hanging on. I only wish those who praise the wildness of wine
could see your 3 ft crawl through glass. One yard of life.

  The tree bears its strains of summer living, reddening
under the long delay of this clear warm Autumn

Spreads out the tapestry of its crinoline skirts

Red rashes on your hands, back and crotch as wine flushes out,
no more a wino, stigmata of the nails. Let's drive a train

without brakes and crash all its carriages in wanton pillage
of dead and dying, of bones jarred from limbs. **It's great**.

Unfreeze ourselves from being driver or passenger. A train
off rails. Not even that. A yard to crawl and crawl back through

the dark room enclosure. On the phone thirty messages unread.
But you walk out, dragging up off the bed, your own Lazarus.

Turning wine into blood
                  wine into blood
any fool can turn blood into wine.

The tree is dressed in rose-red leaves
shedding its poison   red stars

What's beautiful is this curing of itself this flamboyant
leafdrop cleansing   the unharbouring of poison

The tree detoxifying for its own good

The leaves are the colour of rouge the cheeks we used to have when
                                         young
painted by the north light

the room reddens its red walls   Life waiting in the buds

A BREATH IN THE MAKING

Autumn and not yet Autumn. Summer warmth
holds the green in the leaves like an undrunk

glass. Smoke haze from stubble crosses the road
like unsuspected fog. We bike over long shadows
freed from housebound air into a southern breeze.

The river dark under the sun is merely
gliding. It's small here, between near banks,

but ten years have eroded the old path, blank
in brambles. The river shivers like a snakeskin

and on its charcoal sheen only one silver crack
drifts down. The Japanese Zen master of the wind

has chosen a single line to write his poem.

And yet here's another, like breath dying.

Pissarro light stunningly flecks the grass
as if leaves have fallen. We're winged on our bikes

as the sun wraps itself in a muslin shroud,
is far away, ebbing – we're dancing a mutual
ritualistic dance of insects delighting

in false summer warmth, which should be dead
with all those other things: false dawns, false hopes,

or another breath in the making.

THE YELLOW SHIRT

Would it have made a difference, the yellow shirt?
Or the mustard, with thin black telegraph wire
design, treble buttons on the cuffs? You thrilled –

but the collar was too narrow. I saw the discontented
bird of prey that lives in your lips raise one wing
and knew for your not buying of the shirt I would pay.

For staying too long at the doctor's so we both
had to wait, for the storm rain that hemmed in your day,
for the drink you wanted and might have drunk in a secret

pact, for the black bile of your thoughts I have to pay.
The bird of prey is set to strike in the bow of your lips,
in the wings of your lips the bird is hunched, it beats

as you speak, cranking its wings on its steady flightpath,
the flightpath of your insane drone of complaint, it knows
no other job than killing. We might have gone smiling

to the train, you with your shiny bags bringing you
comfort and love couture, I deluded for another day
the bird won't return. I am a cage shutting you out.

SURVIVING LIGHT

anointing the room with crushed glass
the tornover photographs
fractured pictures of you smiling
WRITE WITH A SHOVEL (you advise)

One cup of tea. Talking alone. But I notice sunlight
  on bright green tree trunks and the first pinchings

of pink blossom trying its luck on the first warm day.
  Checked by frost. The roofs' blank slates say nothing.

The page of *Subliminal Light* you almost marked
  reproaches with its rubbed out scar. Surviving

the mêlée of glass grit the maniac squandered
  on the room, smashing fragments to dust, ice pollen,

once protective of us: early pledges, crossing
  and recrossing the Tyne at Wylam under the iron

fan spokes the engineer opened to eyes
  of passengers, the train once arrow to his pulled bow,

defunct as our photographs, the moment of stolen
  present unmistakably the past – the past we shift about

and overscore and sometimes eradicate with a frenzy
  insufficiently total unlike the Gestapo.

Your token signature in cracked glass, one crack
  not enough for your temper draining to the lees.

You left your crystal snail trail in each room,
  and the spoilt pictures will always be in parts,

separated by the moment of tearing memorised by time.
  Your hand cut in the expenditure of dynamite

in the empty house. A small bleeding treasured for its cost.
  Subliminal Light flung and dented. Half ownership

hesitated to mar its tiny paint flecks, trompe l'oeil
  illusion of relief, lighter than mist – the light

travelling like tiny cars seen from a mountain.
  They're all going somewhere or appear to be.

Light curtain of mosaic, a wall of pastel chippings
  hangs in fragments. Fragments clinging together.

Fragments in zero force and zero negativity.
  Delicate equilibrium you declined to shatter.

Subliminal Light: silkscreen print pamphlet edition: James Hugonin

41

WHAT HIS RAGE SAYS

Stubbled, grey-lipped, *I'll smash another cup*
because of flamboyance gone wrong,

in a cell, a cage: my fury rattles the bars,
this casting down, bright feathers blacktarred.

What this rage says: I'm being punished
like Pound under the chill wattage of Pisan

stars, but I'm not a fascist, tasting war
served to me on a spoon, his medicine

intended for underlings. I'm one of the lost,
one of the stolen in the army of the lost,

now in the slave-ship hold in the middle
of the ocean. *Remember me in my Poundian chains!*

And does life measure out to me my measure?
The ones born without arms take their measure,

the baby with one breath takes his measure.
For accident of birth, of health, of life,

breaks the stranglehold of the stars.
Order and chance pair off. We all pay the price,

but some of us, naturally, pay more.
And why am I so punished? Not blaming myself

but blaming all those stars for not being good.
The stars no parent. The universe not watching

with eyes. The sky no shelter. No-one to unlock
my bars. And in these soundings do I find justice

in rage? I cause havoc, but I am the havoc caused.
I am reduced to this shouting man.

Madness unless I remove these thorns from my head.
The blind are led to the cliff edge. I'll thrash,

thrash in my chains. You'll hear the music as mischief
black-edged. And weeping will come, the soul's small

pleas for redress. Strange, how in all this city
of night, *there is one light on.* My heart sings

as a bird in the dead of night, it sings
in song lines of language laid down for me.

Even Pound in his cage lamented in song,
even slaves in the slave ship kept their song,

the Jews through the centuries kept their song
until the Holocaust came down like the last

cold wind on earth to kill all life. *I'll pray*
there were no songs in the camps from the innocents.

ST VALENTINE'S DAY

It was a day like any other. Time for a drink and bragging
and orders. *Be there!* And the jibe loosened upon the air,

I'm not from Warwickshire. You have your reply, O Lover

with your Co-op vodka rogue spirit, lies and unkempt
promises and your stagger. I can smell the wine in your breezy
indifference to answers, the hung-up phone, the childlike

snigger, cough and hiding your head under the bedcover,
the fog of sentences you crawl through and today this
summoning of my presence to Japanese food and hara-kiri.

A drunken lover is the best you can do on this trysting day
but you'll shave imperfectly and wear a fabled suit and
carefully polished shoes. *Warwickshire says No.*

II

A BOOK OF DAYS

April 1999–August 2000

1   *April snow*

You ghost the bedroom and stairs – presences,
cups of tea and talk. Cold conversation.
The trees are blasted. Concrete absences.
I move in Whiteread's *House* of abstraction –
space like trees drowned in the whitest of wash
or a fungus or air of a cement
mill. Loneliness turns this snow to ash.
It's too empty to call grief – to relent
or melt. A ghost stronger in metaphor.
The pale magnolia shades into snow.
I must make my tea, think of a decor
for walls. The underlit April sky glow
is *forget-me-not* of early, airy
clematis blue bells, heads up, shaken free.

2

The silver hall is a clouded mirror –
my choice: *chiaroscuro* of black, grey, white
and silver, blurring light, a shimmer
of moth-grey silk. The walls are so quiet,
they are calm undulations of a sea,
hushing, hushing, Princess-in-the-tower
steps on the new carpet, are not to be
questioned for a flattering answer.
What is wrong with the magnolia tree?
It is curiously orange, petals
discarded like shoes by a refugee,
even buds glow brown as the cold settles.
A massacre of the flowers. Snow drills
its landing parachutes, shoots daffodils.

3

Hurt brown petals uncurl nevertheless,
a slow recovery, the crushed posy
of primroses won't rearrange its dress
until next Spring. Local catastrophe
hits yard. And a Downs baby will suffer
from a change in the weather, a few dropped
stitches in its genes as careless nature
knits and misses. The new-born had not stopped
at the right shops and picked up a complete
outfit. I war all night with cruelty
of life; its haphazard mishaps will treat
no-one special, without morality.
The desperately-tried-for baby cries,
lungs fill lustily as its future dies.

4   *for Peter*

The luck of life, the lottery, the chance,
bestowed on the most innocent: some young
clutching their blotted books of life will dance
crippled, and one grown man groans mis-sung,
his strange unrelieved mind games his brain will
not release him from. Prisoner patterns,
like sonnets relentlessly pursued, till
he is helpless. Has to count his steps, learns
them. *Repeat.* He has to read car numbers.
Repeat. What an artist rejoices in,
curses. Order grinds as he remembers.
First and last, last and first, his white noise din.
Has to sing the tune over and over.
A mind terror he's cast in forever.

5

The calamity of the frost is past
but dead petals scar the magnolia.
We hear on the TV of the bomb blast
and tomorrow's melancholia
will replace grief, lost limbs, faces burnt.
The bridal party met withering
confetti of nails, splinters and glass, learnt
indiscrimination in their dying
and the hidden tragedy in the word gay.
Bride and groom were never to know regret,
their pale blooms opening under May
Eve frost. Hate kills a new Juliet,
and Romeo, under hail by his dead
best man, lies mutilated and unwed.

6

Too dark at 6. I sleep alone and hear
rain, and the emptiness is singleness,
our feet not twinned and twined (your phrase), the weir
of guttering rain is my new distress
bell, waking me to jaundiced pewter light
you love so much, those tender rooftop dove
calls of the slates, when the rain vibrates right
over our bed, its Gamelan above
our stirring. Our love limbs still beat with blood,
our kisses still hang us dangling over
precipices, that long well drop still should
be deeper than any stone discover.
I arise and reach for the phone. It rings
like answering rain. Your voice flutes, chimes, sings.

7 *for Linda on her birthday*

We were cheesecloth girls, *Woodstock* girls, incense
on sticks sheltering us from gnats on your
lawn, our Summers lovesick, poems nonsense,
driftwood drawn on longest beaches, Bamburgh
and Tynemouth – their sea, blue-green eyed with mauve
tinged irises, our accomplice, would keep
secrets. My long thick plait of hair I wove
like a statement of political deep
intent under my black beret, making
love and war, veteran of street demos.
Our laughter was the tree-lodged chirruping
of birds, away from ground hard terse memos
of unhappy marriages. Wars may die
but not dancing to *American Pie*.

8

The *Lie* haunts us, twinkles like a malign
star over a cradle holding a dead
baby. What wise men misled by a sign
will leave gifts? The star is not words unsaid
but detonator from our history.
It's the end of a thousand years, the end
of us at the end of the century.
What can bring back kindness from the unkind?
The *Lie* is brazened out, if repeated
enough it will bludgeon the accuser.
A show trial's banishment is meted
out to her for being prosecutor.
We've lain for years on our bed, Prince, Princess –
was this stone under mattress on mattress?

9

I can't bring my mother back or unkind
brokerage promised to return her book.
You sold truth long ago defending blind
drunkenness as sober. Stories you cook
like Harlem jazz improvised on the wing,
dazzling medley of lies you want tested
like that *canard* of the street seller's sting
daring us to prove he can't be bested.
What's left is the *Lie* that is the snake
around your heart, the guardian of pride
more tempting than truth trampled in the wake
of self-love, self-pity, truth an aside
only whispered in the inner chamber
of a club of which you're the one member.

10   *Two birthday letters*

His last words have calmed the storm, her grave gone
quiet, a voice switched off, as letters come;
dying, he opened the shut tight page, shone
like polished stone with clawing, ancient sum
of unwritten grief, poems never sent
to hers, unsent, diamond tears the world
granted a crown and what she could have meant
to Elysium and history, furled
like wings of a perched dove always above
him, his guilt blazoned, no sword mightier
than a falling feather from a dead love;
dying, he writes answers in deadlier
grief: what he lost he lived every day,
regretted passion like the pearl thrown away.

11

I won't cast myself in Sylvia's rank,
but I think her husband dredged up Daddy
too much as demon, not his love which stank
of foxy wanderings which is Baddy
enough in the book of wife. And why call
her mad? Her despair was ordinary
in coroner's courts. Lives like hers can stall
and start again. I've known the near scary
distance of chance and mischance, the decree
nisi of two suicides, and father
never called Daddy by over-the-knee
beaten or slapped-at-the-table daughter,
but a doctor said my oyster shell pain
of lost love proved I was *horribly sane.*

12 *Four war sonnets*

The Muse of War wakes me flying in dreams,
a vast aeroplane takes off to drop bombs
elsewhere. I'm under its exhausted streams,
its dishonourable signature tombs
the sky for others, and in my head drones
my 1940 phantom bombers; a sky dead
wakes up, while a mad Christian atones
for not being there, watching a child's dread
(true word) alight in the night, haunting me
in the burning orange-red searing dawn
of holiday Greece. Out of that wine sea,
unrecognised fear panicked to be born,
the long dead sunrise of my Leamington
night and Coventry the molten sun.

13

No indignation from the sleeping young
of war like computer games with toy planes.
Nightmare dogs slip with fresh blood on the tongue
from our kennels as the cabinet turns
poacher. Our very young are rotting high
on pleasure, the new god of pills, powder,
the old booze, despised dregs called drugs which lie
of peace while the world is without honour.
Not sick with anger as new Vietnams
fast fire in the drought, leaping from dry bush
to bush, uncivil wars, peace-keeping shams;
after the Cold War, the New Age of Slush.
Pardon the drunk, the drugged, the brained-out dead:
crack troops happy with circuses and bread.

14

The Muse of War shrills as the Christian kills
on nightly crusade. Knights fly unbloodied,
war ethics muddied, safe as cheapest thrills;
something has to be paid for, earned, studied.
Unease. Disgust. Someone paying our cost
in collateral damage, newly born
babies in the maternity ward lost
in undeclared war so-called fighters scorn
to hazard, babies sacrificed to save skins
and politicians who petrolled the fires
of hate and nationalisms. No wins,
everybody loses: the liars,
the cursed, the raped, refugees in shelter.
The war crime is they needed our water.

15

Coventry called up Dresden. Versailles's drum
they were beaten on. And from our clear skies
planes despatch bombs like seeds of Vietnam.
The clear skies worry me, no siren wise
warning, no darkening at noon, no raven.
Take the bomb out of politics agreed
politicians on Good Friday, leaven
in the desert-hard unyielding bread creed
our ancestors baked for a Christian boy
reneging on new dawns – preferring blood
soaked ones to red: new nights, new Coventry.
Young enough to want a quick fix of good
deeds, playing Henry the Fifth on the cheap.
Tomorrow he's the murderer of sleep.

16

My house a ship, sailing the seas of rain.
Yesterday the earth was light and crumbled
now it drinks and drinks steadily, the drain
of a two-month baby who had grumbled
and now gulps metrically. Rain sealing me
inside, intense rewriting of the slates,
violent inspiration mused by the
storm. As I watch, rain's angel hair narrates
a naiad. The yard stones are deep ochre,
polished and pooled, the dry terracotta
face on the wall has its first tears falter.
Rain: director, actor in our theatre,
its own Ariel. Lifting a shadow,
moves on, diamonds and scent on my window.

17 *Being and non-being*

I'm in the bubble of the universe
and it's blooming like a flower in time,
it's blooming and dying, my cells converse
with my mothers and fathers in the lime
flowered spray of the Milky Way – the stars!
Exclamations of being and non-being!
A photon their distant cousin, Mars
and Venus – our brother and sister – sharing
their epic poem, whereas our sun
is a sonnet, you and I its mating
rhymes unmatched, out of touch with their rhythm,
and without their pairing, we are half-things.
Our spaces wait for the photon out of air,
to pinprick, to seed light, out of nowhere.

18 *The Gorgon*

After all these years . . . and he dropped the word
into my gaze. *Do you see the Gorgon?*
He meant my friend, his ex, those Xs blurred:
wife, cook, cleaner, mother, early years one
when fame was still a migrant bird not making
a Summer. What turns all that to blind stone?
The still pretty woman unwithering,
but I've known her skeletal despair crone
her days, days of poverty, homelessness –
days helpless before the brutalism
of Thatcher and her husband's merciless
shedding of crosses, once kisses, a schism
that can rewrite memory, conscience, pain
into calumny, dearest to disdain.

19 *Aneirin*

How calm the expression, controlled the voice,
the three-month-old holds the stage, his lips flute,
no smiles and gurgles now, this is his choice
of sounds carolled to air out of the mute
cacophony of chuckles and cries,
he croons like a cat at greeting, pitched high
and low in eerie syntax, a surprise
of language forming like weather in Skye,
like clouds curling out of the sea, sounds plain
and purl in ancient braiding of a world
before history, older than his name
and poetry, unfurling of his furled
tongue into a lost vocabulary
found on this page of his life's diary.

20 *Newgrange*

A baby is singing like whorls on stone
at Newgrange, the first recorded double
celtic knot etched to show the dead atone
living on, their thread unbroken, single
strand of before and after in a loop
(compression of thought in a symbol) –
bookish monks of Lindisfarne and Kells stoop
in their cells to copy stone-age doodle
burning in their brains and weave on and on
in intricate plaiting the tomb's rebirth –
sounds and signs mirror the continuum,
unbroken thread of life starting on earth,
double helix spiral, the body's knot
copied and copied, plaited, replaited.

21   *The eclipse 1999*

The solar wind is combing the long hair
of the comets, it's whistling through black space,
blowing the nap off the planets to clear
bone. Between this Goliath stands our ace,
our David, our moon, ruffling our seas, holds
winds in check, tempers hurricanes, is small
but nearer, counterweight to solar scalds,
comes between air and fire. Today they fall
by chance like two pennies tossed by gods,
exactly equal in size to our eyes
matched against unimaginable odds,
this tiny stone, this anchor in our skies,
this pawn, this grit, puts out the eye of light
like a little death, like a little night.

22   *The eclipse for Linda*

The sun is wearing a woolly shroud, then
becomes maiden in alluring thin veil,
at her ear a black moon is nibbling when
I run in shrieking, *It's begun!* abseil
into your wall, scraping fingers and arm.
We rush into your garden with pin-holed
paper, eclipse glasses not to cause harm,
but no sunlight. She's dancing with her cold
partner in high mists, we gaze in wonder
as they get closer, black moon checks white queen
until she's a tiara, a slender
finger on his shoulder, flirts to be seen,
(glasses – on – off). Under leaves we capture
the dance of crescent sequins on paper.

23 *The lock and the key*

The drunk glaze shifted out of your blank gaze,
your blue eyes thinned from mirror to window
clear as summer mornings burnt out of haze,
we nursed each other, like foundlings, the shadow
lifted. *We're the lock and key, you and me,*
you said as if finding the key to fit
everything, and you turned the lock free.
We must have drifted in endless time lit
by knowledge, and in our wake like a teem
of light, millions of tiny locks and keys
are fighting spangles in our comet's stream,
hopping about like a carpet of fleas,
doomed to fly and be apart. Rain today
for luck, but no key to the lock of why.

24 *In the glasshouse of the Botanic Garden*

The butterfly fluttered its bow-tie wings,
thinner than silk chiffon, it was a breath
on the air, hovering like a lark sings
above the wind, above the moor, a stealth
of flight like a petal floating thermal
updraughts. Its gauzy wings hummed black and white,
a *Zebra Butterfly*, keen to settle
but unsure of us, this little kite
on the string of our wonder, as we froze,
and it flew freely, a joke of nature,
a drift of magpie in a soft haze,
a bull's-eye sucked to finest gossamer,
flew improbably, a Disney drawing,
tying air into a bow with its wings.

25 *Fall*

September blue skies, the trees lulled, the sun
still hot as news comes, another fall, blood
on the pillow, you wandering alone –
on your first book you pose misunderstood,
James Dean as poet, and angry of course,
Sixties scowl, the poems a young man's rising
lark like Rembrandt's young eyes unlike the Morse
of his last portrait's SOS falling
into the world's silence, the world now glad
to queue in shuffling reverence. Autumn's
a red mist of lice and hospital, mad
DTs which sack your mind like the nine vans
and nine men you saw loot your home. Sober
you find your shelves untouched, your books still there.

26

The worst approaches and reproaches, space
you will drop into as you leap to crash,
that moment beyond my hand as you race
to irreversible madness awash
with drunkenness. You enter No Exit
as the NHS takes the afternoon
off and some too busy psychologist
leaves at 5 and doesn't answer the phone.
We're left adrift, you with your brain about
to blow like an oil well, and me watching
a countdown in days, maybe hours, shout
into the silence of space despatching
your last rocket rise, the burnt out fuel jets,
and you alive gabbling on TV sets.

27

The cliffs of the cathedral are Dover
white, revolving as I walk through giant
doors back into my mind, single lover,
and the one threadbare tree on the ancient
square is welcome for its lack of weeping.
I greet this evening's cold and racing wind
as friendly portent of the earth's turning,
the sober stars blinking, the moon half blind,
none complaining of despair and dullness
and the need for another universe.
I like their unquibbling spare willingness
to be, without Hamlet soliloquies.
Everything that lives unbefuddled,
everything that lives alert, is blessed.

28

I watch you sink in day's ordinary
light, the last star slips through all the meshes,
as in any Victorian story,
but I'm not their heroine sighing wishes.
I'll fight the ending of your last swallow,
a gulp, a plop configuring a pond,
a puncture in pressure of space, a low
hiss into a black hole, all zeros and
your last breath when we add those final Os
right on time for the new Millennium;
it's a cue for a romantic to go,
a *quid pro quo* to end the tedium,
but we're not fast burning stars, we're still on
craggy Earth, a date with 2001.

The paradise of Es Carregador –
sun up like a maiden without riches
in a white frock, mist confusing her poor
attire, flooding sea with silver stitches
now like a million quick fish chasing
hysterically in a net with fright,
swimming the bay on this virgin morning
as she strengthens, blue sky and sea so bright
it blues the coast almost mauve, feathery
bright green pines, cottages, boathouse, encircle;
ash of my mother sanctifies the sea
cast under the eye of the comet. I'll
divide my dust in three, throw me on moors,
Warwickshire spinnies, on Carregador.

30   *Swimming*

Houses were always cold. Alarm, early,
heat never reached my skinny body, rolled
towel under my arm, shivering Sunday
in the tiled Baths as I poorly swam chilled,
and the dawn milkshake in the shiny new
peach and black plastic American bar
congratulating me for getting through
the war and the swim. What survived, not war,
not milk-bar, my joy in before breakfast
swimming, the heady no-one-else-is-here
in silent pools, the still sleeping sea chaste
and milky, only birds quicken before
the day's up. Cold wading into dawn peach
skimming blue. Life left behind on the beach.

31   *Durham bus station (after Shelley)*

Friday night uncages here, a waste land
of untithed charity shops, coal-fouled stone,
gum-pebbled streets dumped on like once gold sand
under 14 ft of tipped slag, a frown
on the coastline under a chain of command
of unending buckets past signs unread
of pollution & global warming, things
masters and miners left to fish, fed
more like a fire, with damp slack, to appear
banked, and when it was all axed like a king's
head, sea, fish, sand, delivered from despair,
the blight bled from mines to towns, decay
all that's left of industry, the once bare
bus-stands a sea scum of fags unswept away.

32   *Funeral flowers for Susan*

White and green: no festivity, blood bleached
out like hope; no holly, no mistletoe.
These paler flowers of snow colour reached
you too late for life – younger cousin go
with your many bouquets, night bride, a star
with accolades; flowers ignite the dark.
Black-shiny hair capped, black-eyed child post-war
in my thin teenage arms, you were a stark
beauty from your father's handsome line.
We took the best of gifts from our mothers –
the Family, grandmother and aunts, fine
women who worked, sang, danced, like troupers:
Ida presiding, Hazel, Bel, Esme,
Stella, Jan, alive in our memory.

33

Flowers for brides, more flowers for the dead;
we deck coffins with barely just living
blossoms, sacrifices, with petals unshed,
cut at the neck, heap their beauty dying,
not tribute to death or the gods but life
itself, that ephemeral spark called soul
or spirit, the life span rainbow of strife
and joy unweaving its colours. We're all
shape-changing from stars to beetles to us
to stars, nothing dies, only alters, quarks
merely, atoms merely, a universe
of particles assembles and a child talks.
The soul adheres, the mind is born to study –
the flower dies but not love or beauty.

34 *Songster*

She was a small singing bird, a young wren
you caught in your hand and felt her heartbeat.
You chose two rings, one for her foot and then
one for your hand. She fluttered like green wheat
beginning to sense the wind, not ready
for ploughing. She flew into the bush and
when you came for me, I saw your greedy
eyes still alighting and smelt the ring band
on your finger. While we were arguing
the two rings fell from your pocket like crows
at a wedding, the giving and wearing
intentional as double knots, zeros,
the two rings plural and not singular,
irreducible in kind and number.

35 *Mourning*

I will mourn the railway bridge at Wylam
trackless, ungloried, the lines all erased –
where passengers could not stop there I am,
a bird in midstream. We strolled among crazed
graffiti urging or warning MADNESS
while you posed us for photographs and raved
of Malevich, called on the bridge to bless
our hearts. Thin, irascible, you craved
visible pledges like a weir marking
fresh from tidal water. The iron reels
spoke of vision, art and engineering,
the two arcs, unridden wheels
of pits, cycles, Suprematists; by these
vowed Incorruptible Love, nothing less.

36 *Kielder Water*

The woods trembled. An incoming storm failed
to rain. Sheltering, we stood close, our macs
breathing, your eyes tentative, your hands brailled
the moment as unreadable, our backs
upright as the firs. They were complaining,
low girning, in their birdless canopy,
moaned like slaves or trammelled livestock turning
engines of unstoppable industry.
Against nature, we agreed, sensed freedom
where a tree's not confined. Territory
was the space around you. We did not come
to the moment which waited secretly.
This was our prelude, the forest's bass cries
the gloom of the firs, your tentative eyes.

37

No-one pities the misbehaving drunk
dying red-faced like a clown, stumbling over
shards of bottles, promises, pictures, sunk
to a level field of dung you think clover,
the drink anaesthetic like the morphine
piped to my mum, last hours flying alone
in her droning plane with a harsh engine,
all of us waiting for her breath to float down.
No-one pities me waiting for the news
I know will come. There's no truth or beauty
surprised in popping eyes as the muse
is taken ill. Fits rack without mercy.
Out of debris your lovely words will rise
singing their Ode to Joy as fury dies.

38 *Testament*

These are your last wishes: *There is only
one place for my ashes. Up a height and
make sure it's raining, above Sparty Lea,
two thousand one hundred feet, the lonnen
head, Dirt Pot. Take a CD up there, play
'Knocking on Heaven's Door', read a poem,
a short poem by Apollinaire and by
you. On the ashes put a black suit (from
my wardrobe. I have nine). My library
I leave to Northumbria, the land
and University. My family
are not literary. But my house and
my possessions are yours. I saw three years
ago in Denton Burn, a solicitor.*

39   *Candlelight*

There is something childish about your flames,
uncertain, like a stammer, you like no
draught about you and firelight shames
your timid puckering, unsexual and slow.
But you have the power to embolden,
to wax like the moon and swell into the air,
when the shy become strong, you are their emblem.
You burn entirely like children who dare
to play to exhaustion. Spent or emptied
of fuel, you can't reawaken, relight
what's gutted and the dregs of what's partied.
In the consequence of losing your sight,
you're the gleam, the flame, which helps us to see,
and you're the smoke, the ending, the not to be.

40   *2000*

The rim of the world bubbles in the glass
of waiting. Hilly Fields is dark and full
of conspirators. Families, prams, pass
over damp grass as fireworks spike the dull
nearly mid-night. Trees bristle the sky-line.
Everyone is waiting. Now. It is
not now. The champagne troubles the brim fine
against the palate of the night while fizz
of seconds die and then explode. The sky
synchronised, pops like gunfire in a ring,
a blitz of fireworks *now*. High blush of shy
new Millennium's untainted fresh spring
is gulped like the first moment a baby breathes.
Always this fresh, this second, as time lives.

Blue and pink dawn in cathedral windows
of the viaduct, pink light blushes pink
blossom, the trees are nerveless black shadows,
a crown of thorns; the New York poets drink
in the 1950s, hindsight is fate,
they chariot their lives like Romans,
uncharted they were young Greeks in debate;
I remember your holy incursions
to the lost world of the Cedar Tavern,
MOMA, and the fame you briefly drowned in:
Greenwich Village could not be found; I learn
by time and separation, the adult pain
of every step in youth's unmapped city,
reliving O'Hara's towers of Arcady.

42

Kenneth Koch and Ashbery still writing,
the rest dead, and you suspect trodden down
by hungry generations who must sing,
nightingales or cuckoos. Chaucer's *House of Fame*
built on ice, one side in sun, one side
in dun shade where carved names are crisp and fresh,
all others melted; I sense the panic of pride
at your missing name in anthologies,
the gifts of tongue, the blizzard of words,
the wanton grace you cannot fall from,
yet they are sliding away, toppled birds,
unsung; *So unfamous was woxe hir fame.*
But men seyn, 'What may ever laste?' So twice
you cut your name, the second in diamond ice.

43 *Snowdrops for Mrs Tulip*

50p chance purchase in Barney – dales
town where snowdrops are hard pressed to push up
frost most nights, the coffin's white-headed nails
bounce out as the new year stirs for a sup,
not dead like wrapping paper the instant
of unwrapping, snowdrops weathering life
unlike my gardening neighbour who can't
come home to her snowdrops and be a wife
to Mr Tulip. No 5 is dark
suddenly, all of us at No 6
wonder at the power of 'flu to pick
and choose. She was homely, kindly, Red Cross
helper taking the ill to hospital,
and knew the place, its failing miracle.

44

Yellowing snowdrops thin as terminal
cancer patients, yellow on the pillow,
yellow as sallow skin no longer ill
after 'flu, yellow after a blood flow
and baby's gone, petals' yellowing pages
or photographs, more umber than yellow,
the yellow more a burnmark of singes
from a hot iron, the yellow not yellow
at all, a sickly orange yellow, neither
orange nor yellow like the glowing fruit,
not yellow like buttercups or wasps or
gorse or the Yellow Pages' indiscreet
cover; that ailing we call yellowing
as if yellow was willow and dying.

45

It's come in a letter, after the fits,
mind damage, the perky liver taken
for a fool or something which always knits
up the unravelled days and nights shaken
in a bedlam of unthreading as if
you're Penelope without Odysseus,
the liver ignored and trusted is stiff
like tearstained paper gone hard, your drunk voice
shouting new anger. I'm *gobshite*, last words
I put the phone down on. February
is the month before the Spring, when the birds
have *Parlements* and courtships, lovers try
their luck. You've run out of love, and choices,
the ninth life, everything but curses.

46   *Ulster*

Between fires the warrior must part
the air. In the lake the sword must be thrown.
Nothing has happened. He's still at the start
of his journey: to let go or to own
the sword and lie to his master, dying,
who wants his power to die. The blade asks
for nothing but to be a blade: killing,
parrying, the metal aching for tasks
by himself. What is strong in laying down
his arm? His story not yet a story,
the sword still on its way between renown
and drowning. What waits is the mystery
of place and timing, not a weapon, more
a vision, surrendering *Excalibur*.

47   *Wendy's phoenix*

So he thought not to hurt her, a little
neglect says so much – about uncaring
cheerfulness when clearly his unsubtle
subtext left her alone, his canny bearing –
lips sealed in a smile learnt on business deals,
says so much like redundancy instead
of a paycheck. But Wend's phoenix steals
a gleam from a new cigarette in bed,
thanks! and a march on the man who forgot
business and pleasure cancel each other –
she's not hurt or waiting for him, she's hot,
he's Aberdeen, Dundee, a cold shiver,
she's Miami Beach, the Caribbean,
he's a North sea, she's the Med, Aegean . . .

48   *The torrent*

The torrent of words, love in the torrent,
hate in the torrent, you'll always be black
& white, twisted, torn, upland water bent
in torture and tempest against the slack
stones, driven by the spring which must run down,
there are no valleys, only hills and rifts,
and the thrashing descent and the long moan
of winds, new rain always arriving boats
of cargo from the seas, tipped on the heights
like darkest slag. There's no escape, the words
must flow. You're on the treeline with the kites,
the old wolf tracks, traced, retraced, round fiords;
becks sing loudest, young rivers in clouds leap
chasms in crescendos, never to sleep.

49 *Second best*

All of us wallflowers, all second best,
harbouring teenage pain at the dance floor
or the unchosen in the team, our breasts
too big or small, too late or soon, to star.
Confessions from matrons. We're just fourteen,
avoiding the plots of parents, too thin
or fat, too frail or wilful, life a screen
not letting us through, except the best one –
target of beeswarming boys, accolades.
Surprised and cheered by this, communion
of also-rans, holding no trumps and spades
instead of diamonds, we are *women* –
wives, ex-wives and a nun, writers, friends,
connoisseurs of words, love & food at Wend's.

50 *Birthday*

A tightening; a gathering, the heart
not an eternal clock, falters mid-breath.
Sweat summoned from the dungeon as it starts
its old car engine, a few notes from death.
The world stands by, made to wait, the driver
idle, at a respectable distance
as the ambulance crew take me over.
Tomorrow Nye's first year is gone, entrances
and exits, we've come through a secret door
in time, I'll shut it when I go, he's spun
out of nothing into gold, and I'm more
the metal of my old Morris 1000,
rusting from salt and snow, whose great heart,
never griped like mine, not one false cold start.

51 *Nye meets sand in Holland Park*

The freedom of it; the newness; strangeness,
tiny fingers grasping what can't be grasped;
knows this is not garden, not earth, not grass,
this is for small underjoyed toddlers tossed
by storms of eating, unsleeping, changing,
racked by pushchairs, sharp corners, falling things;
like the Pope he spreadeagles – he's praying
to the sand god, kisses his pleasure, sings
a gargle of pure love at first sighting,
beatific he dances, tiny hands
open and shut like baby birds cawing
in hunger, he's feasting on divine sands,
senses this is for fun and for children,
eats, tastes, spits, approves with a giant grin.

52 *In the basement garden at the Science Museum*

Another mirage; a water world rushes,
tiny sailors in tiny boats, bob, bounce,
water wheels whir, water spits, spouts, splashes,
Nye, aproned, clings to the edge in a trance,
frantic with joy, strums his fingers astream,
head back shrieks glee, we watch sidelined,
glad he's free of us, the bliss deep, the dream
unadulterated, in his mien
I see my daughter and my son when young.
At home the magnolia is ready
with unlit pink candles and rooms, unsung
with voices, voices, are yet more tidy
but crowded with memories and Spring now
begins with another grandchild *in utero.*

53

You're still alive, I'm still alive, we're at
the same addresses, orbiting a void
where our life used to be, the same but not,
a year on, a year apart, asteroid
we can't avoid unless we move away,
and you're fading to a Cheshire cat smile
of your voice, the last word I hear you say
is love, echoing in the woods awhile;
you'll forget, and I'll forget, pack our goods,
set out our tray of what's used, second-hand,
elsewhere – you need water, I need blood;
we've nothing left unsaid, kind or unkind,
the anxious heart is moving towards light,
what is dark uninvites, the light invites.

54 *Barry*

Love is intimacy, not the perfect
form like ice crystals, or music or death,
not like faith or belief, not the correct
answer to a sum, silence to the deaf,
not inactive like a vase or statue,
not a novel, a poem, a play, dead
and unchanging in their coffins and sure
of their endings. Love is not to be led
on a string of words, netted or petted,
not to be resigned like a sofabed
in a corner of a room, nor strutted.
Love is the quotidian, days plaited,
plainsong, morning talk over cups of tea,
arias & arguments, *intimacy.*

55   *Bells*

Globe-tight, made for bursting, purple-blue sheen
of damsons, the bells plump, thirst for April,
a deluge of pom-poms, the bee-buds preen,
will spring, ring, shout, cartwheel, for loving still.
The bells ripen into *forget-me-not*.
Ring out old spite, ring in new brooms for wives.
The bells will sing of a babe in a cot,
ring out curt tongues, ring in apologies,
ring out dark mills, ring in Jerusalems,
ring out *Mein Kampf*, ring out, ring out, Nazis,
ring in, ring in, Ken for Mayor of London.
The clematis bells are blue wild roses,
ring out blue Labour, ring in the red & true,
ring in gaiety, ring in *egalité*.

56   *Shelley's weather forecast*

A poet's licence with *property is theft*,
you could play so many words in your head,
notes on a stolen theme, the warp and weft
of a dazzling new carpet, tapestried
sometimes from rags. Thanks then for the title
you smuggled into a poem for her,
another phantom muse, fuelling my cycle
with Shelley's leap from ashes to fire.
The Winter come and gone, the sea fret sits
like clouded destiny uncoiling from
its lair of melting iceberg as it quits
the North to spoil the sun, the fog a drum
muffled like a funeral march, ash grey,
not far behind, November cold in May.

57 *For Barry, died 9 May 2000*

Do sheets of the dead-in-waiting still move
on their chest, lift with the tiniest breath?
Yours swayed faintly, as though your heart, your love,
echoed in veins, blurring the edge of death;
eyes shut, lashes down, they trembled beneath
my attentive gaze, the lashes flickered
like a ghostly fairy piano of grief
my eyes were troubling; I kissed your forehead,
nerving for the cold, cool as white china,
your temple become marble, ravages
of thorns under thin hair lovely and finer
to me than tidied under powder; the age
will mourn a poet's death; eyelids, I'll kiss,
nose, lips, with pollen dust of tenderness.

58

You sang in the midden, beauty springing
from your day's conversation, gift of song
unstoppable, distress and bliss singing
descant and tune, it was anger of wrong
and joy of right, plaintive among your *starres*,
plaiting accord and discord. Beauty wins
over dead wars like the single fires
girdling the sky, and they are all one
with us, in stages of living and dying,
changing in the blossom of a speck
to a billion flowers as I, unwitting,
split from you by an atom's check
mate by breath. We'll meet in the circling air
and when unhooped from earth, ignite our star.

59 *Red roses*

Out from the train, black night rain, his face dull
from journeying, Nye is an explosion
of smiles. Home music on, he is a twirl
of fourteen months on feet like clock hands
speeding through time, his fingers shaking high
on invisible castanets, dancing
like birdsong after guns, the birds, like Nye,
inborn with rhythm. We're firelight watching
his small moving flame, torch once set alight
out of milky mire to mosses, now passed
on, a secret code we're spelling out but
not the mystery. An unwelcome guest
at your hijacked funeral, my flowers'
truthful tongues, the only moving fire.

60 *By Cockfield Fell*

Clouds snag across May skies, life persists, rain
feeding the green incense, ordinariness
blooms, the coming child's blinking light disdains
fears, the bud unfurling to witnesses
of fingers, feet, penis, a boy promised –
In the gullies, flowers friends argue about,
childhood names clash, ragwort, campion, red
and white, and what's that? eggs & bacon we shout,
lady's smock, dock, pignut (or cow parsley?)
sorrel (vinegar leaves?) dead nettle, vetch,
field orchid, speedwell, stitched with daisy,
buttercup, primrose, cowslip, violet;
ascension of beauty, time's embroidery,
larks, thrushes, dunnocks, the air's poetry.

61

When we touched, palm to palm, arm on arm, our
souls passed straight through our bodies, the touch learnt
by foretouch in the school of loving for
lost souls still at the desk with can't and won't,
how our bodies taught us simplicity
of giving, no self in the bed, our souls
passed through, all gates open, writing our story
in the book of atoms; there in cold coals
our hot fires will be read, quarks and sub-sparks
met and exchanged histories from the bang
of time, our wavelengths were singing the talk
of love into silence, and your eyes sang
with the choir of it afterwards; when we
touched, it sprang back, a reflex of that sea.

62

Days are the seconds' hand of the year's clock,
days tick us on, make us forget what time
it is, forget to read the hour, the shock
of what we're doing, where we are. The rhyme
and rhythm of days lulls me. The pattern
not read while forming. It kept its secret
until closure, I'm prisoner, slattern
of indolent days, of minicab debts
of tiny journeys, of impersonating
bishops with a solemn drone, or pronoun
queens pronouncing 'us', how I am missing
your caustic hiss, you read me with a frown,
noting faults with charms: *how do you cope*
with angel wings considering their scope?

63 *Midsummer*

We haven't learnt to shuffle the pack of time:
the card dealer deals the cards. I wake up
on the longest day, not from a long dream
on Christmas Eve, before 'flu; before hope
of Millennium cures died in Greenwich,
the hospital not Dome; before the flight
in a cab to your fatherland, Shoreditch,
Isle of Dogs, snapping at your heels, the white
line wobbling so much you rang from Hackney;
before you fell down Marks & Spencer stairs;
before you cracked your knee in February;
before my heart nearly quit its career;
but if tomorrow was Christmas, would we
rewrite our love, our days, our history?

64

We form abstract ideas: truth, beauty,
justice, in a republic of the mind –
and our senses are working hard for duty;
the idea survives the thing, your hand
squeeze on my shoulder is remembered for
the signal of your love: *take it easy*,
as I battled the non-fixer of my car,
who blatantly declared the new wheezy
exhaust should backfire, bang, burp, fart, cough,
to be expected, the outrageous claim
I shot down with my fighter plane guns duff
until you steadied me and I took aim.
My hand replied to yours in secret code.
Touch is gone, what's left, the accord and bond.

65

An idea must form like life itself,
something from nothing, like the universe
from a seed so small it vanishes, wealth
becoming negative equity, worse
than zero, niggling a sense of balance
into being. Everything is changing
into ideas, present into past, chance
into fate, life into history, string
into rope, small ideas and larger,
and the gods of truth & beauty & justice
will linger when we're no longer matter;
where's love and hate? good and bad? virtue, vice? –
the things we do, not aspire to, the things
we are, when singing changes into song?

66   *Holiday reading*

I jump from bed to catch the sun, smoke grey
burns rose, I'm late, the sun already up –
streamers of gauze cloud hid a chink of ray –
she's an opera star in veils or fur wrap
as I wait for her to preen, book in hand,
Mahon's homage to decadence and yellow
under her hot light – (no quarter found
in nature!) – he fears no heroes, mellow
endings to centuries of spite, desire
becalmed by healing, and cares to forget
the poet as shaman with a muse of fire;
in extremis you wrote in a dark strait,
child killer, Lucifer, Hitler, no respite
in your moil: *'but I'm going for the light'*.

III

THE WORK OF THE WIND

for Hazel Litherland

THE WORK OF THE WIND

In his late evening Miró sends postcards.
In his late last day the sun and moon share haloes,
are sinking and rising,

scattered on the waters of the air.
The wind pays his calling card.
The last visitor has come to clear all debts. Clear

all the poetry of a life into a last tumble.
That's the work of the wind. The moon and sun of a life
bouncing to the edge. Stop at the edge as they fade.

Raddled and sieved. All the work of his life
raddled on the barbed wire of the wind.
It comes to last messages on postcards.

What can he say more than *Sun & Wind, Drowned Sun,
Moon & Wind, The Work of the Wind II and III?*
Everything is clear. Everything is over.

The sun and moon hold their histories
and their currencies. Suspended by the wind.
It comes to penetrate, scatter and cleanse,

rifling through dust, shaking it off the page.
We're down to last heartbeats advising us.

The sun and moon, father and mother,
son and daughter, lover and lover.

All taken by the work of the wind,
air waves of motion, moving us on, changeling
matter, cold energy, unfocusing us.

The black moon falls and fights like a whirligig,
a burr snagging time, catches in the fabric,
is furious ending like a crossnibbed fullstop.

The last whisper, the last breath, is the wind.
The ego sun enlarges behind the wind curtain.
Red in death. The wind turns on its side into rain.

A LILY

for Rachel Ben Harry Nick

       The last breath   not the last breath
her face white and worn   not shrivelled
thin ribbing of mouth we have lightly sponged

with tiny sponges on sticks   her breath
pumped and pumped in regular harshness
by her heart in charge   overseeing

the last race to the tape. And I see her
hands thrown up as she breasts it   the way
they do on TV. Except they stay at her side

thin under the sheet and single blanket.
She breasts it with a slowing breath.
And her eyes are opening. They are pearl

and silver unseeing. The lids slowly rise.
Rise as slowly as legs lowered in exercise
to flatten the stomach or flags lowered

for the dying. Rise slowly enough for me to say
Quick get Harry who is outside watering flowers.
We hold her hand   or the sheet   the five of us

who have risen one by one from our beds
by the quickening rasping. The vigil keepers
in a row crouching close with their farewells

called like passengers on a liner seeing
the land move away. And now the breath
is light   so light I want to catch it on a mirror

like Lear for Cordelia. The nearly last breath.
And another fainter and longer and nearly the last
breath. We wait and here's another so soft

it barely stirs her lips. It is so important
to know when it is the last. And it must be
for the opal pearl eyes have opened   and there

isn't another. Her face utterly unchangeable
from the moment before without another breath.
And when the others have gone I hear the machine

give a last whine. Maybe there was a silent other.
And the bedclothes maybe I can see them move.
I stare and they appear to move. They lift and sway

in their stillness. *She is like a lily*
says my daughter. Perfectly white and still.
The last I will ever see of my mother. The face

in the coffin   the waxen stern face is not my mother.
She is this tender skin   these unpressed
fading petals withering as death blows out

her breath. I close her weightless lids
on opalescent moons. We scatter into the garden
as the sun is rising. It must be slowly rising

strongly rising and turning the hands of time.

YOUR LAST NIGHT

for Hazel Litherland

Your harsh insomniac last night called us
out of bed to the steady coma drone
that would not let you fly off or come down
in your lonely plane. Reminiscences

criss-crossed the blacked-out sky, of Christmases
and Charades, the old-fashioned talking one
with dressing up for acting scenes, the fun
improvising: when we were the ladies'

string band going down with the Titanic;
then you a dog under my old fur coat
on hands and knees growling with a stick.
We laughed and laughed – and your sick, remote

engine switched off your plane's idling, its sights
toward the runway set out with Christmas lights.

TWO SCATTERINGS

for Rachel, Ben & John

I *Harbury, Warwickshire*

Not grey gritty ashes in a plastic bottle, but spirit
we throw from this Harbury hilltop, childhood landscape

in my head, the primrose woods, the bluebells tied
on the back of my bicycle, hugging the Fosse Way,

revered as iconic spine of Warwickshire
touching no town from Stowe to Leicester, now a fast

link to the motorway. This hilltop windmill, sails
permanently stilled, does not respond to the strong

wind as we cast your ashes like seedcorn to the air.
The air which pulls up the dead weight like a kite trailing

dust, your comet's tail, the veil lingering
like silence after music or reflection on an idea

or the moment of response when someone hugs you
and your heart warms. Again and again we throw soft chintz

hangings of ash carried unknowably to Warwickshire.

A skylark, itself a dot, appears above us. We hear
fast twittering, locate the speck hovering from its invisible

cord. High spirit, *holy dove*, blesses our flings

to flight your ashes. The grey evening lightened by wind
is cold, beautiful, with no-one in sight. The windmill

frozen in time, its clock hands stopped, is ornament,
gravestone and marks this site with a giant cross or kiss.

II *Es Carregador, Mallorca*

The sea, morning pale blue, merely trembles, a glazed sea with
early sun, watches us walk the tiny rocky shore and well trodden

path to Es Carregador, the seaweed thatched bay with its
ancient tamarisk still untroubled by time, past the inlets

where storm rubbish collects, civilisation's shredded
blue and black plastic, to the clear unvisited headland

we call the mountains of the moon, a cratered span
of rocks and trapped salt pools drying into crust.

We clamber to the outcrop finger point. We want the furthest
and somehow the nearest to the vista of the coast. From here

we see your beloved walks through pines, the bay we taught
the kids to swim in, the cottage *La Esquina* where we sat

wet-clad to eat the breakfast of *ensaimadas* and jam
from your own apricots made just for us and the holiday.

Antonia entering with a flourish with her delivery
of fresh tissue wrapped sugar coated shell light and

shell shaped pastries. *Saïm* is lard in Mallorquin,
she explained this time, without you. Except the other

container of ashes here, in sight of all kind and unkind
memories. No Sontags in the house on the rocky shore

where we sat on the new concrete spray buffeted
patio built just out of reach of the worst winter storms.

And my father is somewhere on the hilltop still waiting
for the slot he lost in the reordering of the cemetery

and his only memorial, the house he built from hope and fear,
beloved *Madroño*, rising on its deep stone wall, is in

others' hands, and others walk the tiles he and you chose,
look through the windows you tested in England by

measuring upward from your seated chair, the very rooms
planned and replanned, the roof lost in the first gale,

the drive lost in the first rainstorm, all resurrected
to form the perfect home on blasted rock, adored *Madroño*

once visible from the outcrop when it stood alone.
All your days encompassed, and on this calm, well performing

sea – laying down its least ripple to bear your ashes
thrown onto its silky just breathing motion sucking at

the rock edges – we cast as far as we can into the not windy

brilliantly clear azure sky, the grey ashes turning
to gold in the water, magically glittering like gold specks

in the underwater sunlight, drop glitteringly down to the
golden underwater rocks. We cast again and again and the veils

of ash hang over the spot like smoke from fireworks, and in
the sky that night, the four thousand year journeying comet

is a singular thumbprint among the sharp stars, a blurred tail
of ice we see as light. Marks the month of our propitious

casting to the unforgiving gods of memory, time and loss.

GRANDMOTHERS, GRANDFATHERS

Warwickshire bred us, mother, daughter,
father, and further back long dead

grandmothers, grandfathers. The Litherland one
proudly his own man delivering coals

on his back as merchant sprung from pitman boy
entering the Griffe Colliery at 11,

and by 21 out, never spoken of again.
Warning his son: *Get a trade* to live, for respect,

fear-driven, the need to rise above his station.
My father into the factory at 14, toolmaker

apprentice, nightschool with his bible:
The Mechanic's Handbook with its thumbnail index,

everything in there gold text, somehow the answer
to everything. And grandmother small and old

in the Home for Incurables. The long boredom
filled Sunday visits, asked to play in the gardens

outside and then brought to her briefly
like a presentation at Court, hand trembling

bedridden, taking tea from a spouted cup,
hardly known as I kept my well behaved place

and never spoke until spoken to. My allegiance
to my mother's mother, the true matriarch,

thrice-married with a bevy of children
all dotted around Warwickshire (aunts and

one uncle who was in disgrace), Ida, who had loved
not wisely but well, on her own and working

as canteen manageress among the big steel pans
and smells in Birmingham's great firm,

Stewart & Lloyds, maker of tubes, all sizes,
and so the story goes: it was sent one day

the smallest tube in the world by a rival
in America and returned the tube with a tube

inside. Grandfather Clem, deserted for a roving
sea-captain, was the weak one, who at 21

had his proud début as solo pianist at
Birmingham Town Hall, and then was stricken

by sleeping sickness. His palsied hands only
fit for serving in his family draper's shop

and for teaching piano to cane rapped children.
I remember his dogs, Alsatians kept in sheds,

and his second marriage idiot son wandering
under the damson tree, retribution

not wished on wicked Auntie, stepmother
to my mother and left behind sister and brother.

The Witch who never let my mother clean her teeth,
who cut off her red curls and tried to make plain

her beauty, who punished & overpunished
with deprivations and Puritan hatred,

who called the missing Ida: *The Scarlet Woman*.
Who my mother met secretly outside school

and when at last the schoolgirl went to work,
she ran away to *Her* and returned triumphant,

first pay packet all spent on a bright red
lipstick, high heels and cherry bobbing hat.

ANEIRIN AND THE SEA

He is singing his world into existence,
the baby is crooning, not simple *agoos*
but a long discourse, his eyes, the first eyes
of addressing the audience in waiting.

He has learnt people croon these sounds
to each other, these long singing phrases,
and nod and smile and gesture. Not only people
he speaks to in their first language before

words, he is changing his world into sound.
This first ever naming, trapped in a baby's
mouth in fossil crooning, halfway between singing
and talking, this Ur-language faithfully

kept in the books of his body, encoded,
recorded. Aneirin sings of the world and sings
to the world. Next day we present him to the sea.
The sea is casting noises on the shore, crunching

water with a heavy beat, returns and lingers.
The sea a melody, the first music, the crooning wind
talking as wood talks, the pram on the sand
hushing, hushing, and clicking and clicking,

the dog rustling his paws; air thinly vibrates
with gull swoops and gull call, we are chatting and
laughing, catching words in a ball and tossing
back, the world is ariel, aural, all spaces

resounding. I show Aneirin the sea constantly
moving itself, and think the ancients were right,
stars must be singing in the high register
of light. At home Aneirin reports to us,

translating his three-month-old world, his eyes
concentrated on this, his first poetry,
for poetry it is, half talking, half singing,
a reincarnation of first sounds

in the first people, the world emerging
into words not yet words, phrases not yet phrases,
yet phrased and strung, this precious necklet
not yet a necklace, and wonder catches us

wonder catches people, *So young and he sounds
as if he's talking*. Aneirin is crooning of the sea,
of paintings on the wall, of floating
conversations, of the inborn when it was born.

DARK MATTER

The unlit ones, the unborn and never to be born,

not in our glittering arms, the spiralling
outflung, out-spinning galaxy arms all strung

with faery lights, the dazzling solo dancer
of a galaxy, so we thought, slim as a disc

on end, a plate of stars spinning in the universe
one of a billion billion and still counting on.

But we're just a hot fiery core unloosening
and spinning with switched on stars, and the rest,

our brother and sister gases out there, our
extended family of nebulae never advancing, our

nest of dark matter, are the necessary left-overs,
the might-have-been stars who attended the gala

but don't get to sing. We're part of the show,
part of the chosen, our dot of a dot of a dot,

somehow managed to snuggle itself next to a sun
one of the minor kind, in those trillion flickering

lights, in the not-to-be-explained necessity
of combustion and burning. We always believed in

dark and light, and we're part of an invisible
ball, part of the lightning skein through it,

the dark galaxy ball we never suspected, spinning
and heating up until the centre's on fire and

we're in the coils of the burning wire.

THE GLASS MAN AS EXHIBIT

The skin is made of glass. We see the skeleton
through glass. Hitler's perfect man. Its perfection now
  mute appeal, its glass skin
a body without skin. We see right through to bone.
Let's carry it out to the street, to the weather.
  It can stand in the square
  where they can't decide on
a memorial for Jews who lost skin and need glass.

It's been granted a blessing, a benediction,
time alighting on those uplifted arms, become
  a singular irony,
a ghost in glass. Time a busy clerk recording
the stories, truth emerging from the mud sighing
  to let it go, fragments
  of the impossible,
blown into air, grease and ash, are gradually

reforming. Kounellis's room of smoke shadows
left by flames. Whiteread's concrete air preserving books
  like teeth in dentist's clay.
The carnival of carnage, nude pageants, love of
uniforms and snooping (written by themselves as
  heroic), their tiger
  attention to detail,
detail become claws, their dancing in the tiger

skin, when history stank with their sweat for a while.
Time is all we have to exalt the Innocents.
  We grant them the thrones.
They are assembling in the light of millions
of stories, inheriting memory, their ghosts
  honouring absences.
  Let Hitler's perfect man
stand in the square for Jews who lost skin and need glass.

Yannis Kounellis: installation artist
Rachel Whiteread: sculptor of the Holocaust Memorial in Vienna

THE CONCEIT

You aren't here to see the windowbox
of coral geraniums brighten in the grey
and one flowerhead quiver

under the weight of a flying-in
blue tit poised on swaying blossom
like a conceit in Chinese embroidery.

LILIES A FROU-FROU

Nothing maidenly. These are taffeta skirts
of the cancan dancer, not legs kicking
high but fangs of sexuality, burnt gold hooks
like radar bleeps crossing the mind of the bee.

And what of this knobbed stem dripping
a tear of honey. How blatant and uncovered
like mating when sheets are tossed off,
these starched petals peeling back, saying

take me, I'm a marvel of gorgeous life
and sternly arresting of the bee's flight,
he's not sucking so much as sucked in this
tangle of golden thorns and jab of the syringe.

Those raised ginger brows, those stiff pennants,
that dash of bitter in the white lady cocktail,
stirred by the stick in the drink you offer.
You don't wait for your skirts to be lifted.

You arch, there's display in the white scrolling
petals, curling with that last moment of desire,
out of the shade of your pale green heart,
your matching elegant stems hoist chilli peppers.

ENGINEHOUSE NEAR BURNTHOUSES

Photograph by Pat Maycroft

The Enginehouse stands in its winter,
windows black, unslated roof, strands

of beams like thin strands of hair,
the snapped-off downpipe, rainwater

left to trickle down stone, unhaunted
ghost house, beautiful in its once life,

heart and work gone, an abandoned
house weathered to ruin; and slowly,

gale by gale, waves of weather strip
and pick the bones; the Enginehouse lives

through love of shape and form, poetry
at work, the obliging snow, trick of track,

bristling winter tree at a field's distance,
hedge of cobweb & eyelash; we know

this Enginehouse, this old-age, remote,
rarely visited, gaunt, yielding & unyielding,

the engine has moved out, life has moved on;
the poetry remains in stony resistance,

in sky, snow, treads, tree and stone all
silent as a moment of prayer wishing for something

to stay and last, as even stone will level
and retreat back to earth, under landscape.

IV

INTIMACY

February 2000–July 2001

I

The air Icelandic,
   creaks of old frost giants,
is also prophetic.
   Is it beauty, or the planet's

future we're ignoring like pages without writing,
   not seeing what's not said or written or read
is also a warning?
   White frost is the crisis of tongues dead,

the planet coming to the boil
   may switch streams,
and the lid of ice denude the surface, art scraped off like soil,
   the jeered at history, litter-thrown

boulevards, the already lost forests and creatures,
   life a nearly blank page,
ice deleting my walls of silver,
   my lounge strewn with an impression of leaf-fall by the old age

of my carpet,
   the awaited frilled petticoats of my clematis,
the thousand years of cathedral on the parapet,
   libraries, galleries, cities,

tabula almost rasa,
   seas of ice drowning Europe, Asia, the U.S. and Russia,
life a kamikaze
   raid on the going nowhere good ship *Utopia*.

On my table snowdrops,
   a gift of friends,
diminutive plump petals opening like tiny mops,
   they'll survive where the ice ends,

where moisture makes life, meet
   snow crystals in an argument of beauty.
We can't compete
   but what they may lack is intimacy.

II

Strong winds on the Long Sands
    pluming the sea, the waves' spray backcombed,
even the puppy waves could not run in as the tide intends,
    the wavelets ruffled in their paces and alarmed

as the sand's columns attack in formation,
    the topsand drowning,
the wind playing sand devils lost in action,
    wind & water & shore interchanging.

People jostling backwards and forwards in quick turns,
    a ball makes sense of their rhythm,
lunges, darts, spurts, feints, spurns,
    defending, attacking, families in a schism

of happiness and a shriek at *goal*,
    their energy all about fierce freedom,
 the game has the movement of a shoal.
    Walking on a long strand in Greece, a beach no-one would come

to even in Summer, like stretches of Northumbrian coast,
    we idled, my son and I, having swum
uninviting freezing water for a dare and boast,
    and thought of cricket like a sum

in need of an answer,
    picked up pine cone and driftwood for ball, bat,
and the game had no spectator,
    until our third day returning to our spot,

a boy stood some way off,
    with something like hunger.
Cricket on a lonely Greek beach, an oddity to scoff
    at, misshapen bat and make-do ball. His wonder

real, he asks to play as if we were an oasis
    on these sands, a drink of water
cool to parched and thirsty lips, bliss
    to an Australian boy transported here,

and with the nearest thing to intimacy
    the three of us played for an eternal hour,
and if football is a game like drama, cricket is poetry.

III

I'm talking distinctly,
    quietly, as if to a slumped pilot
in a plane with little fuel. He's too high,
    his path tracked by observers, a cursed Lady of Shalott

with his cracked mirror and cracked voice,
    'in love' with something once: *'enchantment'*,
and knows he's in a store of no choice,
    on every shelf, in every department,

only one thing on sale, like a Russian shop
    when Gorbachev fell, people buying what was there
to keep the feeling alive, queues did not stop
    when stores went empty and came to stare

at just one shoe left on the shelf.
    Enchantment a future gone bust
the truth a notion of stealth
    like unwatchable pitting of metal to rust.

He's in the time of racks & racks & racks
    of bottles gleaming in his Aladdin's cave's mind
polished by desire to highlights. I prise open the cracks
    in his singleness of attention and can't find

his thoughts, he's slumped but listening.
    He's been up too long
and is flying
    with nowhere to land, his flightpath mapped like a song

we know will end. You're not *'in love'* anymore I say.
    I'll talk you down out of clouds and air.
It's hard to say goodbye to intimacy,
    the cargo must go first, the stash in your lair,

look at the dials, they're all wrong and there's a red light
    on, whatever you feel, you're spent
not spending, like the Russian people left in the night
    wondering where the dawn went,

the dawn we thought a promise,
    crowding the boulevards in a sea of habit,
not believing the emptiness,
    an unforgiving sea of disenchantment.

IV

Stamped in the violet
    in the heart of the pansy,
its mark, its panther face set

    inviolate, a statement of being we
know won't change like your incurable
    defiance, a singularity you have drunk yourself

into and adhere to, unable
    to detach yourself
like a stamp from a letter not addressed

    or going somewhere. At heart
you're amiss, keeping loose, impressed
    with wantonness, promiscuous cheat,

true to yourself, and it's almost to be admired,
    pursuing the aching muse,
the reinvention of love inside your head,

    a necessary seeking, why then accuse
your flowers of opening these late days? Flowers
    although meddled with

are inside our lives and outside our laws.
    Caught in the death
of this spiral, unfavoured star collapsing

    to memory, you are held
by your craving
    to be free of anyone's telling, a wisdom too cold

like charity. I recognise the crucible of your marking
    and marring, defying the stamp of authority,
authority without intimacy.

V

Dark music in the doctor's,
    surgery, my face grey and sweating,
the head untethered feathers,
    the heart crushed and crumpling

like a half-finished thrown-away poem
    on its way to the bin,
sent back for rewriting, take this as a black omen,
    the arrival of the raven,

stress the traitor within my gates,
    fifth column posing as caring,
the world appears to me a choppy sea of stress with my little boats
    all struggling

to be in harbour,
    and what if over-weighted stress,
like orders heavily breathless, always **Do this** father
    to child, is him always shouting: *a mess,*

you're making a mess, to a dog or a cat or a daughter
    and there's no cure only thrashing,
and the thump of squealing from puppies and kittens,
    and sitting on coals in the coalshed and not giving

or giving in, anger laments
    in dark music, stomach cramps and stuttering,

the forgotten unforgotten torturing of small things to obedience,
    the litany, the long litany of hits and slaps,
sticks and banishments; Kim, Alsatian pup, who didn't dance
    to the right tune under whips,

baffled by orders, dying of a brain fever,
    Simon, springer-spaniel, who was given away
to be spared from cringing, his liver
    and white livery shaking, and Whisky,

the indomitable cat they tried to kill
    but the vet set free, came back to sit on coals
but would not enter the spell
    of the house of scolds;

and what if stress is lifelong intimacy
    of the raised hand,
flinching never removed from memory
    of a quickly averted face and voice of command?

VI

27 Lee Road,
    in my dreams I'm gardening its stubborn garden
of rough grasses, planting borders, a hedge braid
    instead of the post-war wire fence, warden
against street cricket I'm not allowed
    to play, a princess in the tower
without long hair but I shinned
    down a drainpipe, my own deliverer.

No books on the shelves but my precious
    Children's Encyclopaedia by Arthur Mee
with royal blue covers, my father, lathe operator, anxious
    to improve me,
wanted the best. He loved machines and engineering,
    the delicate poetry of the *thou'*
the discipline of precision, jeering
    at the untaught, unskilled cow

of a workforce he'd escaped from, in his balloon
    of night-classes, his destiny: tool-making, cars, machine shops
& management, his moon:
    be his own boss & he was practising on us with belts.
My father's thin blue lips
    – he had a heart condition –
pressed together in heavy disapproval of all quips
    never arising to mock his authority. He smelled of pickled onions,

his voice the cutting edge of the lathe,
    shouting, practising mastery, his temper
schooled me. I was in a school of his awakening, expected to be
                                                    brave
    & unspoilt, to work harder
than my friends, and always mute, well drilled at table;
    knife and fork correctly held
correctly placed, unable
    to match the perfect form in his head –

if I faltered, I was bruised by the flying hand that expected
    like Nelson my duty.
The order said,
    demanded, the right action to a *thou'* without an error's frailty.
It was wartime,
    planes bruised Lockheed factory with bombs,
to let locked-in light escape from our windows a crime,
    the sky alive with barrage balloons and alarms

like the wail of a animal who has been hurt as a pup.
    After the All Clear, the intimacy of the stars
so close to earth, so many pressing towards me, a daisied-meadow up
    -turned, like snowflakes always arriving, older than wars.

thou': machine shop term for working to the nearest thousandth of an inch.

VII

What knot can't be unwoven?
  Nothing my brain can't unpick
after tests I was given.

Small child tied up, hands behind back,
  ankles together, trussed and put in a room.
Houdini trick. My father timing.

I would work at those knots with all the wriggling my brain
  could devise. Eel, water, anything fluid, rippling
under constraint. Out

through the hoop of my hands to whittle
  knots like a stick, to cut,
loosen with teeth and spittle.

The rope slipping,
  and, like something returning to the wild,
sprang into its fatter shaping,

was on my side. Hands once freed,
  red roughened, pulled like some birth of intimacy
at cords, tore at the feet, seconds

of frenzy,
  the knot a smashed lock springs undone.
The legacy

unerring fingers pluck
  entangling string or chain into harmony
from discordant music.

Tests of geography lists,
  capitals of the world,
tests of mental arithmetic

suggest feather-head panic and blindfold
    fear.
My father intent on measuring the weather with barometer,

tapping for storms and calm, trapping the air
    with a max and minus thermometer,
frustrated scientist, engineer, cricketer.

I wonder at his bequest,
    as I read my son's gift, a year's
sub of *New Scientist* and watch all five days of the Test.

VIII

The raised hand,

    the raised voice,
always raised levels & levers of command,

    always the orders, the disapproving advice,
always the water in my head fermenting,

    the avalanche of water that cannot get over the waterfall,
bashing and thrashing,

    I won't clear as a bell
rings heavenward, the All Clear on madness

    of planes in my head, the droning bombers,
the always war between parent & child, he's my sadness,

    my enemy, my Germany.
The stricken waterfall igniting,

    Hitler newsreels hoarsely screaming hate.
Incendiaries of Injustice burning

    hate-glimmers in my heart,
Führer voices, the German nation

    ordering and under orders.
Injustice on fire will drench Dresden.

    After wars,
I meet the Jew

    we didn't protect from the self-appointed perfect race,
with masterful voices and whips and the drive to follow through,

    but we fought the voices with the grace
of a perfect *No* to command,

and Europe a graveyard of resistance –
always the Furies of Injustice singing without sound

the purest of notes, mother-cub protectors of innocence.
The intimacy of Belsen, the walking bones and looks

of abandonment, the cages opened, and what was unspeakable
kept mum and recorded in books

of silent photographs on the coffee table.

IX

Red-orange daybreak growing in the North at black night
    under the hours' long raid, wives & husbands in the shelter
hiding deep fright,
    the knowing dread of bombers

on course, sky armada.
    In my green siren suit with matching pixie-hood I'm sleeping
                                   and waking,
bunk beds tiered like shelves in a larder,
    the women knitting, the men weaving stories like netting

to keep the sky from falling. The paraffin stove
    crocheting a jacket of steel over the soft light puckering,
smelling of safety, the light nesting like butterflies above
    on the cement ceiling.

Intimacy without windows,
    close as a heatwave's airless night,
open to the sound of bombers (not ours),
    a heavy locust cloud humming without number, unstoppable
                                    blight

horizon to horizon. *Someone's getting it.*
    The Scheherezades fearful of ending their stories, told on and on
until the All Clear brought us out,
    painted in sky, painted in sky-blood, firelight shone

on our faces, on my siren suit and hood,
    the North red, tips of flames like thorns,
our fear ashen as we all stood
    like a watcher who mourns

on the road back to Pompeii,
    returning to storm clouds of Vesuvius,
the red haze, black hail of boulders, eight miles away,
    – swift mouth stopping orange molten lava in a surprise rush –

as the crow would fly, but would not in that burnt air,
    and still burning levelling sea;
in such a whirlpool of fire
    sank Coventry.

X

Tangee Natural,
   only the stain of a blush on my lips,
a stick of pure orange, I can recall,
   like plastic, but would paint the pink of rosehips

crushed to syrup, it was all the rage,
   that, and pressed powder
clouding my nose and cheeks in a stage
   mask of pale fright risking the attentions of my father.

Face chastened in the cloakroom of the flicks,
   I thought all traces of *Natural* and fake
despatched in a quick
   splash, for the sake

of the evening inspection,
   his eyes appraising my rubbed cheeks
and lips and reflection
   of my fear unwashed with the rest. Weeks

of life in a moment sweating, and in the heat,
   in my pores opening like flowers,
the scent of powder and paint;
   he sniffed close, like an aged bee that wavers,

on track of a close-by fragrance,
   his eyes magnified to scrutinise a trace
of colour, however *Natural*, unnatural by chance
   of lingering perfume, unknown to my face.

Not sure, he ordered a wrung flannel,
   just in case, and scrubbed my cheeks and lips,
in a vain trial,
   to crush the indelible *stamina* of secrecy,

my lips drubbed to red more like the rosehips
   flagrant on the hedgerows, tender as intimacy.

XI

A ghost at your funeral,
  my roses pricking air with blood of grief,
unwanted guest in the aisle,
  Christian air laden with belief
and hypocrisy, friends, family,
  others, sang their tunes
without intimacy,
  my heart in secret runes.

Bunting's May blossom
  on bridal hedgerows and here the dirge of tears
for the coming season,
  your not-voice shears
the stone from stone, the groove spelling our
  not-love, your body burnt,
eyelashes, tufted cut eyebrows & hair,
  your mouth, your small hands (undipped

in that lake to make them fair), slender shoulder span and chest,
  long legs, downy arms with the bracelet of watch,
my hand you pressed onto your heart when we couldn't rest,
  our bodies' quotation marks,
your eyes searching the weather
  for signs, eyes at bliss after love,
our souls passed through each other,
  palm to palm, the conduit gone, the body burnt on its stove,

all that space around atoms lost to ashes,
  the not-holding arms,
the not-recognition of our faces
  at the bookstall, your home
barred like a prison with your family warders,
  your black suits, T-shirts, orange baseball cap
from Cuba, somehow regain through your letters,
  and the dead pressed flowers, the vibrancy of your sap.

My roses debate whether to stay
    or rush to the river,
the rendering down of a life, a body,
    love burning to a cinder,
leaving your love-words always tremulous,
    always fearful of our parting, always
pleading, pining, avowing: there'll always be us,
    fresh like the grass.

XII

Waking at six,
    out of a trough of sleep, we feel blessed
by absence of frets,
    sighs, turnings, it is morning and you're dressed,
up for a cuppa, this our talking time,
    you prop the bed-end, we bemoan the world's failing
& read a poem, light enters in rhyme,

    the red room brightening,
your ankles under my caress.
    Our mood not sombre,
we rant mildly,
    your Harris Tweed coat taken to the cleaners,
the buttonholes came back like eye sockets
    gouged by a demented Regan.

You'd sent up rockets
    of outrage & amazement but no compensation
for once. You went for papers, hunting for buns,
    while I dozed in our morning, free of nagging
chemical smells on the pillow. The intimacy of the sun
    in the window. The gate clicks, flagging
your return. The day shifts to breakfast,

    warm croissants downstairs,
on the table with toast,
    smoked salmon and coffee and the day's cares
exclaimed, safely exploded resentment
    and a joke about your love
of rain. You stand outside like a smoker, intent
    on looking for clouds and sniff what isn't above.

XIII *Es Carregador*

In the single bed of my cell,
    before sunrise grey light of rain or England,

then the first golden bar on the well
    quiet walls sings.

I open shutters of *La Esquina* to the sun
    rising over the palest of pink haze

and mother-of-pearl sea, plumb
    on gold-leaf path to the rocks craze

cradling the dangerous corner of shore
    road below

this tiny front terrace, cement ladled floor,
    lights the writing table where I am widow,

cassette tape of your words by my bed,
    your long vowels

in the unsleeping hours in my head,
    naked and fresh as swimming I rise to, like chorals

at May Morning in Oxford.
    The sea is satin.

And I think of you writing in isolation, the words
    sent from your clinic: *The matin*

mist is rising to greet its lover
    the sun. The intimacy lifts my grey grieving,

the heat of light on this paper,
    my writing travelling like a boat across the virgin morning

or myself swimming the flarepath
    sealing the vault of half

my mother's ashes (half in Warwickshire
    to stay with childhood and Harry).

Yours, from the fire,
    seized by your family, not allowing one crumb to carry

from the table of your body
    for me to cast as loving hail and mist

upon the lonnen head at Dirt Pot above Sparty Lea
    as you wished.

These words in recompense,
    scattered in heavenly sun,

the sea flickering tense
    with sparks, as if golden rain splashed down.

XIV

The lost house,
    aubrietia at the gate, your gran's lilies
of the valley from Sparty Lea, the full blown blouse
    of the flowering privet, gillies,
unhacked bushes, the wild herb garden,

    the hosepipe trailing, the once mown lawns
gradually abandoned, a Forest of Arden's
    thistles and pear-tree blossom, lilac heroines
in the thicket, the apple tree cankering
    above our once sharing of MacNeice and Yeats,

comparing drums and tides,
    before the threshold crossing of hearts,
IKEA rug, glass table, we chose like bride
    and groom, cutlery, lamp, changing
of interiors, new shelves, Mr Elliot's

 patient joinery of doorway and chimney, arranging
of pictures, and tiny white blots
    stapled on our faces from paint rollers, the row
in B&Q, and making up in the car park,
    weeping over an aria on the radio,

the house of courtship, fitful ascending lark
    of love, night terrors and confessionals,
house of our pledges, first tryst and marriage
    bed, your bedroom's sunniness, the trills
of ice-cream vans, harsh words' damage

    repaired in morning breakfast trays, love an offering
of peanut butter and jam,
    New Yorkers in Denton Burn, the house of suffering,
of flights, avowals, the house where I am
    banished from one last look

at where you tethered your dying body,
    but in my mind you cook
on, the stews with herbs, make Blue Lady
    tea for us, waitered out to the patio
we had set over weeds and rock,

    intimacy the ratio
of loving to loss, where you lit the lamp,
    crowned me queen, boss-babe,
not up for sale or repossession stamp
    of your family who forbade

my mourning last glimpse of your ending,
    in contravention of your key

still on my keyring,
    our seven years unlocked in my memory.

XV *Borrowdale in Time of Siege*

for Linda Saunders

We've scrubbed our boots, wondering
    at the simple buckets and brushes
to protect the hills from our feet plundering
    the flocks like outlaws, trekking past bushes

of untrodden fern and bracken, to this cleft
    in high pasture, this female fissure
of waterfall and pool hidden in the weft
    of the grasses. We undress in high Summer,

there's someone in the valley piping
    like a shepherd or Pan, trills
of an earlier England with sheep crofting
    beneath the eminence of hills.

The water is lean and lovely,
    we curve into it, up through the dark channel,
warm light above the cold deep intimacy
    of the stream, gliding through the steep tunnel,

widening into the pool against the flow,
    the sky stark blue, the valley bright green,
England in simple dress. The pool below
    the shawl of waterfall, we swim to preen

its feathery boa about our necks,
    hand on crack we haul against the throw
of spray, gasp and clutch on rocks,
    against the beck's full pregnant bow,

the bubbles up to our chins like rising laughter,
    two women nesting in the foam,
then let go, riding the swift water
    like a sudden decision to run home.

Nothing sacred here, we eat sandwiches
    and snooze on this borderland meadow,
pipes play on, under chill banks midges
    keep to their underworld dank shadow.

We re-enter like lovers for a second desiring
    of the moment again, the cold ripples
we curve through, it seems a second coming,
    another stinging with the waterfall stipples.

The sun outlasting our leaving as we wash
    boots again of their markings and the choice
of this valley, this day, in a rinsing splash.
    We dipped into the same water twice.

ACKNOWLEDGEMENTS

A number of these poems have appeared in the following magazines: 'Lily', *MsLexia*; 'Poetry as a Chinese Jar Moving in its Stillness', 'If I Only Had Someone to Protect Me', 'Lilies a Frou-Frou', *Tears in the Fence*; 'Red Dawn', 'Spartacus at 5 a.m.', *Fire*; 'The Yellow Shirt', *Smoke*; 'Unwritten Entries', 'What His Rage Says', 'Roses', 'Tangee Natural', 'The Lost House', *Sand*; and on websites: The Poetry Society, Durham Writers, Vane Women Word Web.

Sonnet 34 *Songster* from *A Book of Days* won a Commendation in the National Poetry Competition 2003.

'Grandmothers, Grandfathers' was commissioned for *Private People* (Self Portraits in Verse) to celebrate the tenth anniversary of The Collective Press.

'Enginehouse near Burnthouses' was inspired by a photograph of that name by Pat Maycroft. Both appeared in the anthology *Northern Grit*.

I would like to thank New Writing North for the 'Time to Write' Award 2000 which allowed me to complete the first draft of the manuscript. Five poems from the *Intimacy* sequence, III, VI, IX, XI, XIII, were published in the Award Winners anthology, *Catalyst*.

Fire magazine printed Sonnets 57–61 in a Barry MacSweeney memorial issue.

Six of the poems were selected for *North by North East* (Iron Press) anthology of North East poets.

Vane Women Press published a postcard of Sonnet 22.

Each poem in the sequence *Intimacy* contains the word 'intimacy': an idea borrowed from the New York poets.

'but I'm going for the light' is from the MS of *Blood Money, the Marvellous Secret Sonnets of Mary Bell*, sonnet no. 93: Barry MacSweeney.

Sonnet 66 *Holiday reading* refers to *The Yellow Book* by Derek Mahon.

Note for *Intimacy* XV *Borrowdale in Time of Siege*: Foot and Mouth epidemic required walkers to disinfect boots at special cleansing stations.